Charles Prentiss

A treatise on the scarlatina anginosa, and dysentery:

And sketches on febrile spasm, as produced by plogiston

Charles Prentiss

A treatise on the scarlatina anginosa, and dysentery:
And sketches on febrile spasm, as produced by plogiston

ISBN/EAN: 9783337730307

Printed in Europe, USA, Canada, Australia, Japan

Cover: Foto ©ninafisch / pixelio.de

More available books at **www.hansebooks.com**

A

TREATISE

ON THE

SCARLATINA ANGINOSA,

AND

DYSENTERY;

AND

SKETCHES

ON

FEBRILE SPASM,

AS PRODUCED BY PLOGISTON.

By ISRAEL ALLEN, M. D.

LEOMINSTER, (MASSACHUSETTS)
Printed by CHARLES PRENTISS,
FOR THE AUTHOR, & ROBERT B. THOMAS.

1796.

TO THE

FRIENDLY PATRONAGE

OF

PHYSICIANS

THE FOLLOWING

OBSERVATIONS

ARE

Inscribed,

BY THEIR

MOST OBEDIENT

AND

HUMBLE SERVANT,

THE AUTHOR.

Sterling, *October* 1, 1796.

A
TREATISE
ON THE
Scarlatina Anginofa, &c.

The general Type of the
Fever.

To characterize this epidemic by any particular symptom or set of symptoms, would be difficult. In giving the history of the disease, it will be necessary to mark the different degrees of febrile heat, and general type ; and notice the variety of symptoms under particular cases.

In general, the presence of an inflammatory diathesis prevailed, but in various degrees.

Excess

Excefs of febrile Heat.

IN cafes of high excitement the patient is accompanied with many difagreeable fenfations ; as head and back ache, throat inflamed and very painful, the tonfils tumefied, eyes inflamed, fkin hot and itching to excefs, naufea and vomiting ; the whole vafcular fyftem greatly excited, and the action of the extreme veffels very much increafed : all thefe fymptoms, united, form an affemblage uncommonly irritating and diftreffing.

Thefe fymptoms generally terminated at the completion of five days ; but if the difeafe anticipated a crifis only, the fymptoms on the fixth would go on increafing ; but fhowing figns of crifis ; as a partial moiftnefs on the fkin, turbid urine, &c. and a final folution and relaxation appeared evident at the completion of the feventh ; at which period, the body became fweaty and moift, the urine precipitated a fediment, the tongue cleaned partially, and there was a more free difcharge of canker from the throat, than had happened

before

before. A lively delirium, quick pulfe, hoarfe-
nefs, an apparent atony, vomiting, fometimes
purging, large difcharge from the tonfils, were
all attending fymptoms ; but a perfeft crifis
conftantly happened to thofe under this form
of difeafe. The patient being freed from the
violence of excitement, generally remained
feveral days, very fleepy, feeble and deranged.

Defeƈt of febrile Heat.

AS it is of importance in practice to diftinguifh the different degrees of febrile heat ;
fo in this diathefis it is neceffary to mark the
different ftages of difeafe. Two periods are
peculiarly dangerous, viz. the time of acceffion and receffion of eruption. The danger
at the beginning of difeafe evidently arifes
from want of aftion or mobility in the extreme veffels, and an obftinate fpafm ; thereby occafioning local determinations to the
brain and lungs ; this defeƈt of reaƈtion, and
the danger, are greatly increafed by the coin-
cidence

eidence of cold, being received juft at the time
of acceffion, and a conftitution favoring febrile fpafms and fpafmodic affections. The
patient, very foon after being feized, becomes
ftupid, has a fmall and frequent pulfe, obfcure
heat, fometimes vomits and purges infenfibly,
the eye fixed and glaffy, the refpiration foon
becomes anxious and difficult, the tonfils mild-
ly inflamed, fome fmall inflammatory pimples
in the throat, and imperfect eruption on the
neck and ftomach. With thefe alarming
fymptoms, the patient generally dies within
the firft twenty four hours, unlefs means are
employed fufficient to excite and increafe the
mobility on, and determination to, the furface
of the body. Many livid fpots have appeared on thofe who have died in this ftage of
difeafe ; which fome have thought were from
a broken and diffolved ftate of the blood ; but
I apprehend the appearance was from an inflammatory diathefis, determined to the fkin,
and violent febrile fpafm.

Patients that have been relieved under
fymptoms

fymptoms like the preceeding, and a final folution of difeafe, obtained, have (on taking
cold) been feized with a fecondary fever, and
blood taken away has conftantly appeared
fizy and inflammatory, which it would not in
fo fhort a period, had it been broken and diffolved before.

Receffion and imperfect Crifis.

THE period next to be noticed is that
which follows the receffion of the eruption.
This period, in this form of the difeafe, the
practitioner ought to keep in view; and is
between the fifth and eighth day. In this
ftage and form, prognoftic is dangerous. The
patient has no unfavorable fymptom, the fauces are moderately inflamed, the heat equal
and mild—no derangement of the intellectual
functions; finally, every fymptom promifes
fafety to thofe unacquainted with the complaint ; when, unexpectedly, the patient becomes

comes infenfible, the eyes inflamed, an acrimonious faliva difcharges from the mouth, an
acrid mucus from the nofe, very eroding to
the fkin, and a fanies from the ears; the face,
neck, hands, and feet bloated, the tonfilar and
parotid glands tumid; the action of the heart
and arteries feeble; the natural warmth, or
vital energy perceptibly diminifhing, and every morbid fymptom tending to the fatal period; which, few cafes excepted, is rarely more
than forty hours from the change of fymptoms. All reafoning refpecting this fudden
change of fymptoms, would be hypothetical;
but, we may however conjecture, that the
caufe, or particular ftate of atmofphere, which
originates the fever, is highly active and ftimulant; and by reafon of violent ftricture, or
expofure to cold air, determines to the fenfu-
ous part of the brain. And, confidering the
fuperficies is an expanfion of blood veffels
and nerves, and greatly inflamed and irrita-
ted, may it not be alfo fuppofed that the plex-
us choroides, and pia mater, are inflamed
early in the difeafe; and in the fecond ftage,
the

the medullary fubft..nce is inflamed and intire-
ly diforganized? Local inflamations of mem-
braneous parts, we are affured, are not attended with high excitement. Whether the change
arifes from the caufe fuggefted, or from an
abforption of acrimony from the glands, is
not known.

I have never obferved, even in one inftance, any local determination under the firft
form of difeafe, where the crifis was com-
plete, except what was common to both, a
forenefs and fwelling of the joints. But when
the tongue retained its caft, the furface continued dry, and other fymptoms of doubtful
crifis, till after the feventh day, a receflion
followed, and a particular determination was
evident. In one inftance, it evidently determined to the brain, and produced fymptoms
of an hydrocephelus internus, as might plain-
ly be traced, by the dilated pupil and other
fymptoms correfponding. In another inftance, to the inteftines, followed by dyfente-
ric difcharges. And in a third to the lungs
                                        and

and bronchia with fymptoms of fynanche trachcalis. A fourth determination, and which is common in an obfcure crifis, is to the parotid glands, which continue a long time indurated, after the ulcerations on the tonfils, uvula, and mouth are abated and healed.

Secondary Fever.

ANOTHER charaĉteriſtic in this difeafe, is an aptitude remaining to febrile heat. Cold air, wet cloths, rooms, linen or fhoes, quickly renew the inflammatory diathefis. Thofe in a ſtate of convalefence, muſt cautiouſly avoid any expofure for ten or twelve days at leaſt, after the crifis. Wine, fpirits or tonic medicines, muſt be adminiſtered with caution. The fever that follows is very inflammatory, and renews all the preceeding fymptoms, except the ulceration of the throat. A boy who had the complaint, with the ufual fymptoms, except the eruption, grew tired of confinement,

finement, efcaped to the barn ; the following
evening, a delirium and febrile paroxyfms,
great heat and efflorefence fucceeded ; the tonfils inflamed, greatly, but without canker.
The fever raged five days, when a favorable
crifis appeared.

General Remarks.

SOME peculiarities characterize this difeafe, which are not obferved in any other
eruptive diforder.   I could never be fatisfied
whether it was contagious or not.   At one
time, when it entered a family, one only would
have it ; at another, two ; at another, all.   At
one time, it appeared to follow in a week or
lefs, after being expofed ; and at another, not
till after four or five ; and many had it without ever being in any way near an infected
perfon.   The efflorefence on the fkin is not a
certain fymptom of difeafe ; neither is canker ; and many had neither an eruption, can-

B   ker,

ker, nor fever ; a fore throat only ; at the faine time and fame family of which three died ; a circumftance, that it was the fame diforder. In one inftance it appeared local, as no other fymptom happened, but inflamed tonfils, which continued feven days, attended with a large effufion of faliva, the quantity of three pints or more in twenty four hours ; a circum-ftance, likewife, that it was not a common fy-nanche ; four others of the fame family, the following week, were violently attacked with the difeafe. A free difcharge from the throat was a fign of fafety, and the reverfe, when it could not be promoted. An abforption was fucceeded with tumefaction in the glands, ulcerations in the nofe and ears, an obfcure heat and debility. I have never obferved any general tendency to putrefcency. The ulcers in the fauces were deep and very offen-five, before the crifis ; efpecially, when the patient had been neglected or taken tonic medicines too freely. Cold and heat were equally to be avoided ; heat increafed the reftlefsnefs, anxiety, and febrile irritation ;

cold

col 1 gave a fenfation equally unpleafant. Cold and hot drinks had the fame effect as the temperature of air. Thofe with an excefs of diathefis, parted with their hair and nails; thofe with lefs excitement, the fcarf fkin only. Thofe under the higheft excitement were the moft debilitated, and remained convalefcents the longeft. An abforption to the glands in many cafes was more troublefome. Many, under a mild diathefis, had as perfect a crifis, which was as diftinctly to be traced, as thofe under the higheft.

From the 1ft of March, 1795, to April 18, 1796, one hundred and fifty perfons, moftly children, had the difeafe in this place; and eight of thofe died, viz. One on the 21ft day, emaciated with conftant heat, large ulcerations and abfceffes in the inferior part of the throat, aphtheous mouth, and general acrimony of the fluids. Two on the 9th, from imperfect crifis, and an inflammatory determination to the brain. One in twenty four hours, from violent febrile ftricture, on the furface,

furface, and a determination to the lungs and bronchia. One on the fifth, an infant, with fpafms, and dyfpnoca, at the receffiòn of eruption. Two on the 7th, from cold, after an apparent crifis ; the natural and vital heat being repelled ; the contractile power of the fibres being feeble, a general atony and tumefaction fucceeded. One by local affection of fever exerted on the inteftines.

Indications.

ALL that medical aid can do, is to obviate the morbid tendencies, or local determinations to important of vital parts. Heat, the only known ftimulus in nature, when an excefs is received into the fyftem, by the lungs, from the atmofphere, or by abforption, or in contagious principles in the air, or be detained by cold, and an excefs is accumulated, increafes the contractility of the mufcular fibres of the heart, and the furface of the body. The

The increafed action of the heart increafes the velocity of the fluids, and while the refiftance on the furface continues, a febrile effort commences, and continues, till the action of the heart overcomes the refiftance, and an exhalation of heated fluids takes place; or the refiftance called reaction repels the heated fluids to the brain or fome vital part, and deftroys its mechanifm.

The indications are two, viz. Remove the caufe, excefs of ftimuli, and obviate the fatal tendencies. The peculiar tendency of eruptive fevers is to the furface. The fcarlatina exerts its influence on the tender furface of the fauces. Many writers have fuppofed the particular determination and inflammation there, producing ulcerations, were the moft dangerous fymptoms in the diforder. Debilitating the veffels of the throat, while the fpafm continues, by poultices externally applied, hot fumigations, and relaxing gargarifms, augment the fuffufion and inflammation

there

B2

there. The indication to obviate the morbid tendency, is to repel the heat and check the violent action of the inflamed veſſels by aſtringents, early in the diſeaſe; and after the parts are greatly ſwelled, ſtimulants to obviate loſs of tone in the veſſels.

Method of Cure.

AN emetic in the beginning generally relieved the patient of many painful ſenſations, as nauſea, pain in the throat, headache, &c. Immediately after the operation, I ordered the fauces to be gargled, with a ſolution of ſugar of lead, alterrating every three hours with a ſolution of ſalt water and vinegar; at the ſame time directed the external parts of the throat to be bathed with the ſame ſolutions. The determination to the ſurface, the next indication, was promoted by internal and external means. A febrifuge medicine, compoſed of nitre camphire and golden ſulphur

of

of antimony, was given every three hours, alternated, faline julep, and tincture of opium, fufficient to take off an excefs of irritation. The bowels regulated with glauber falts and caftor oil, or rheubarb and falt of wormwood; a gentle operation only, being neceffary. Bathing the legs in warm water, poultices to the feet and blifters favored the indication.—As children cannot ufe the gargarifms, the nurfe ought to touch the tonfils and other inflamed parts with a foft fwab or armed probe; wet with the aftringent folufions. This courfe, varying with the fymptoms and indications, I continued till the fifth or fixth day, at which period the inflammation was at its acme. At this time I changed the courfe, ordered a ftrong folution of borax as a gargarifm, in brandy and water, and gave fpirit of nitre, camphire and opium, as a febrifuge. After the crifis, which may be expected on the feventh, I have found a folution of white vitriol in rofewater the beft aftringent to prevent a return of ulcerations and aphtha. Much caution and attention is

now

now neceſſary. The nurſe muſt conſtantly aſſiſt
the patient, if a child, with the probe, to dif-
engage and diſcharge the canker; and particularly to preſs the tongue down, and exam-
ine, and diſengage that which lies lodged on
the tonſils. Some patients have not ſwallow-
ed during the night, from inattention of the
watcher. I have been obliged to paſs a large
armed probe between the glands before the
patient found relief. The teeth and lips are
to be frequently waſhed; and the throat like-
wiſe, before eating or drinking. At this period of diſeaſe the ſurface of the mouth and
throat is tender, and dry; the patient can only whiſper. A ſpoonful of ſome oily medicine, after waking from ſleep, is very uſeful
indeed. In this ſtage, the bowels are to be
opened, if neceſſary, and reſtrained if a di-
arrhœa be urgent. The patient can neither
bear evacuations nor tonics. A middle courſe
is to be purſued, gently reſtoring and nouriſhing.
Here, I would remark, that I have never ob-
ſerved any eſſential benefit, from any vegetable aſtringent, nor from allum, gumkino, nor
from

from marine acid. I would alfo inform my readers that I made trial of Dr. Sims' medicine, recommended by Dr. Bulfinch, which is the vitriolic acid diluted with water, and think it the beft aftringent in ufe. The few cafes which happened after I received his publication, do not allow me to recommend from much experience, but have no doubt of its efficacy in this and other inflammations of the throat. After I was acquainted with the medicine, I employed it with fuccefs ; it is aftringent, ftimulant, and antiphlogiftic ; the laft property perhaps is only local, and the effect of the aftringent.

The Dr. prepares in the following form : take oil of vitriol from one to two hundred drops, pro re nata, fpirit of lavender eight drops, fimple water eight ounces, united together in a phial, which he directs to be given, a tea fpoonful or more, every three hours, and ufed as a gargle till the fifth or fixth day. The Dr. cautions againft ufing it too freely, left a ftricture be induced on the lungs. The fame

..fame caution is neceffary in giving bark, while the arid fkin and inflammation continue. This he depended on for cure except neceffary laxatives to regulate the bowels.

The indications in an obftinate fpafrn at the acceffion, are to increafe action and mobility. The method, which has afforded the moft certain relief is either partial or general fomentations; that which is the moft convenient, is foaking cloths or flannel blankets in hot water, falt and water, or vinegar and fpirit; and which muft be applied over the whole furface, and often repeated, till action and reaction are increafed. Internal ftimulants and antifpafmodics muft be vigoroufly employed—as volatiles, mufk, ether, camphire, infufions of faffron and fnakeroot, &c. which may be given warm and often repeated. This courfe if taken early, before the refpiration becomes difficult and laborious, has often reftored reafon, and recalled to action the vital principle, which had been almoft fufpended

pended. As foon as the determination to the fuperficies is reftored, the fever affumes its ufual type.

A large blifter to the back part of the head is very beneficial, if applied at an early period. Emetics are hurtful, not being fufficient to overcome the fpafm; the nervous influence and mobility of the fyftem being greatly decreafed. Cathartics increafe the fymptoms. Bleeding, performed on a young man, by a phyfician greatly embarraffed with the fitua tion of his patient, gave no relief; he died in thirty fix hours.

Friction with moift hot cloths has been found very falutary.

I would here beg leave to introduce an idea, whether fome preparation of tobacco might not be ufeful in this ftage and form of the difeafe, as well as in other fpafmodic complaints.. A refpectable phyfician from Canada* informed me he had ufed an extract of
tobacco

* Dr. RAYMOND.

tobacco for the cure of colic, which had not
failed in one inftance in thirty years practice,
if exhibited early in the complaint. The following recipe is his form of preparing it.
Take tobacco, fenna, and anife feed, of each
two ounces, boil them in water to the confiftence of molaffes, add cathartic fpecies, fufficient to bring it to confiftence for pills; as
fcammony, coloquintida, aloes, and rheubarb,
equal parts. Two pills of common fize
were generally fufficient to eafe the pain, and
operate as a gentle and fafe purge, in an
hour, or at leaft in the ufual period. It certainly has fingular effects on the fyftem; it
difcovers fedative effects without affecting the
fenforium, or deftroying the periftallic motion
of the inteftines. Dr. MAY, alfo, in an in-
augural differtation, has demonftrated from
experience its antifpafmodic power, in teta-
nus, when opium failed. Patients in this form
and ftage of difeafe, are fo delirious and com-
atofe, I have never ventured to give opium;
but on the Brunonian plan it certainly would
be proper. Tobacco, having the antifpafmodic

modic power, without the fedative, has the preference in many cafes, and I have no doubt of its being ufeful in febrile fpafm.

Indications and Method in imperfect Crifis.

WHEN the crifis is poftponed, to the end of the 7th day, and no relaxation is obtained, with little difcharge from the glands, fkin dry, mouth aphtheous, any prognoftic muft be hazardous. A remiffion, however, takes place about the fixth day : but if no fweat appear, nor other marks of folution, we may prepare for difficulty. If low delirium, ftupor and mental derangements, come on, we may fufpect an abforption of acrimonious fluid has determined to the brain ; and in every inftance I have feen it has been fatal, whether to the brain, inteftines or pleura. In one cafe only, where the crifis was put off till the tenth, no local inflammation followed.

From the feventh to the tenth I gave tonic and ftimulant medicines, as bark and fnakeroot, firup, balfam, and fpirit of lavender, fpirit and water more freely than before ; fufpecting that debility was the caufe of the fever's being protracted. On the evening of the 10th, applied two large bliflers in addition to others, and gave an emetic ; a general fweat and ufual figns of crifis were obtained. A tumefaction, in the cellular fubftance, appeared in about a week, which I apprehended was the effect of the tonics ; but it might be from abforption. I gave an emetic and cathartic, and an infufion of tincture of fnakeroot, Guaiacum, faffron, and Peruvian bark ; which obviated the atony and fwelling in a week or thereabouts.

One determination from imperfect crifis remains to be mentioned, which is to the parotid glands. Thefe cafes, before the period of receffion, appear under the flighteft form of the difeafe ; every fymptom favorable, and the patient unwilling to be confined. An

enlargement

enlargement of the glands, obfcure heat, ul-
cerous throat, gums, lips and tongue; pulfe
quick, countenance pale, general ftate enfee-
bled. Thefe cafes are commonly attended
with worms. The indications are many;
as, emetics, cathartics, blifters, fudorifics,
friction, and tonics after the heat has fubfi-
ded. The heat continues a fortnight or more,
and the debility for a long time. The real
and effential indication is to invigorate the
fyftem; but I have not found it poffible, while the febrile and foul habit continued.

All cafes of this defcription terminated
favorably at laft.

Indications in a Secondary Fever.

ANY expofure to cold air, damp rooms,
&c. expofes the patient, to an inflammatory
fever.   The

The courfe to be purfued is antiphlogiftic, as, bleeding, puking, purging, bliftering, &c. which may be employed, according to the age and particular ftate of the patient. A crifis is generally obtained about the fifth day.

Obfervations on the Dyf- entery.

SINCE the commencement of the year, the following diforders have been epidemical in this place, viz, the chicken pox, the hooping cough, the fcarlatina anginofa, and the dyfentery. The latter of thefe began in auguft, after four weeks of very hot, and dry weather.

The caufe of this fever is a precipitation of the fixed air, from an excefs of phlogifton in the furrounding atmofphere.* The heat being

* *The exhalations from dried brooks, &c. being water decompounded, and arifing from putrifying animals and*

being particularly exerted on the inteſtines, produces an increaſed exhalation, and diſcharge, and an immediate tendency to mortification, eſpecially in young children.✝

The ſymptoms at the acceſſion are, head-ache, vomiting, thirſt, alternations of heat and cold : theſe are followed with ſevere gripings and dyſenteric diſcharges. In the economy of animal life there is a conſtant tendency to putrefaction, which is increaſed with the heat and moiſture of the atmoſphere. The principle of vitality which put the machinery in motion, and has influence in continuing life, in every inſpiration, becomes, when increaſed to exceſs, the principle of diſſolution. Every fever

vegetables, are very noxious and produce the worſt kind of dyſentery.

✝ *The abdominal viſcera and muſcles corrupt the ſooneſt of all parts of the body after death, and the quick putrefaction here may reaſonably be aſcribed to the putrid ſteams of the fæces.*

(HUNTER.)

C 2

fever is attended with danger, and thofe in particular, in which the heated perfpiratory fluid is locally feated on a vital part. Thofe which arife from atmofpherical heat and contagious exhalations, difcover a rapid tendency to putrefcency.

The cure of dyfentery, being a local inflammation, and arifing from heated and contagious air, muft always be doubtful and uncertain.

The indications are to take off the fpafm on the furface, and moderate the heat, irritation, and ftri&ture on the inteftines. For taking off the febrile ftri&ture, ele&tricity has been recommended and employed with fuccefs ; but as this cannot be always convenient, the furface may be relaxed, and the ofcillatory motion of the nerves on the fkin increafed by fri&tion and warm bathing, daily repeated, till the ftri&ture on the furface and fpafms of the bowels, give way.

At

At the acceffion, gentle emetics are much to be depended on, both in refpect to the ftomach and the febrile ftate.

Laxative purges, * demulcents, and acefcents are to be employed till the inflammatory fymptoms fubfide. As a laxative, a folution of Glauber's falts, and tartar emetic may be ufeful ; or when that cannot be retained on the ftomach, an infufion of rheubarb, Englifh faffron, and gum Arabic ; or fal rupellenfis ; being more agreeable, to fome,

and

---

* I am informed by a practitioner in Pennfylvania, that the may-apple is a very valuable cathartic in dyfentery and colic. It is a plant about two feet high, grows fpontaneoufly in the woods in Pennfylvania, Newyork, on Mohawk river, and upper Canada. The leaves refemble thofe of coltsfoot, or wild grape : the apple is of the fize and colour of a lemon, of an odorous fmell and not unpleafant tafte : the root contains a large quantity of mucilage, and when boiled to an extract, becomes a gentle, but certain purgative, operating without giving pain or irritation. This plant I take to be the fame that Dr. MORSE calls mallow-indian phyfic, (Spiræa trifoliata) page 172, edition of 1793. I hope to cultivate the plant in my garden the enfuing fummer.

and equally ufeful; with the addition of caſtor oil to either of the foregoing forms, if neceſſary. As a laxative, on thoſe days the purging medicine is not employed, either ipecacuanha, waxed glaſs of antimony, or tobacco, may be given in ſmall doſes and at proper intervals; the latter is very ufeful either in powder, or extract. As an antiſeptic; an infuſion of columba or golden thread root; * the latter, I think, is to be preferred. To finiſh the courfe for the day, a doſe of thebaic tincture may be given at bed time, if the fpaſms, teneſmus and diſcharges are ſevere; which is to be preceeded by warm bathing and the application of a dry warm flannel to the bowels and ſtomach. The moſt uſeful demulcents, are gum Arabic, iſinglaſs, and fweet elm bark; † the latter of theſe, being put into cold water, becomes an exceeding agreeable demulcent, and gentle laxative. Allowing, in every ſtage all kinds of vegetables, and ripe fruits, which contain ſubacid or ſaccharine

* *Nigella.*

† *Ulmus Americanus.*

charine qualities, as apples, pairs, mush and
water melons, &c. and even onions and cab-
bage, have been found fafe and falutary.
All cool and acefcent drinks,as imperial,whey,
buttermilk, cold water, apple water, barley
water, brandy and water, &c. &c. The diet, .
chocolate, coffee, tea, milk, rice, &c. I have
always obferved children at the breaft, bear
the difeafe better than thofe who are weaned,
which induced me to direct milk; and as many cannot bear it in its original ftate, cream,
water and loaf fugar boiled, make a ufeful
fubftitute.

In the fecond period of difeafe, after the
inflammatory and putrefcent fymptoms are
obviated, aftringents, tonics, demulcents, and
animal food are to be employed ; and through
every ftage I have experienced great benefit
from exercife in the open air every fair day;
and for children, geftation on a horfe or in a
carriage, if it can be fupported, is very falutary. I have feen children recovered, by exercife in the laft ftages of weaknefs; even after

ter aphthae * and other marks of putrefcency, had appeared.

Ventiducts may be kept open into the apartment of the fick during the night and day; frequently wafhing the fick with cold vinegar or fpirit and water.

As a preventive to this diftreffing difeafe, I know of no one thing which would be fo ufeful as cold bathing. Many children fall victims to the heat of fummer, who might be faved by cool purges and bathing, efpecially thofe lately weaned, who are very liable to the complaint. And it is to be regretted there are fo few baths in this country, convenient for adults—efpecially in feaport and other large towns, *where* the quantity of air is greatly diminifhed. Should health and plea-fure appear objects fufficient to arreft public or private attention, it is hoped houfes will be erected both elegant and ufeful ; and for-cizners

* *Dr.* Simms' *medicine is a ufeful gargarifm, and an-tifeptic in this ftage of the diforder.*

eigners no longer complain of our inattention
to an excercife fo agreeable and healthful.

A Review of Practice.

THE pathology I have given of the Scarlatina Anginofa may appear to fome very in-
accurate; but not more fo than the difeafe itfelf. It appeared in various chara&ers; but
I have attempted carefully to mark its varie-
ties, and various tendencies—and as it difcovered an inflammatory irritation, but in different degrees, I have partly adopted the antiphlogiftic courfe. As the complaint was fta-
tionary thro the fummer, and operated moftly
in autumn and winter; I have found the bark
and other tonics increafe the heat and canker
in the throat, and general ftri&ure and dry-
nefs on the furface. What has been the type
of the fever in the adjacent towns I have not
been informed, only from common report.
To prevent a violent effufion on the tonfils
and contiguous parts by aftringents, and ob-

D   tain

tain a crifis as early as poffible, have appeared
the chief indications. In 1786, the Dyfentery
followed the Scarlatina Anginofa, as an epidemic, and many perifhed. The difeafe in
many cafes was not under the control of medicine. In the prefent year it has appeared in
the general charaƈer, and in a mild form,
proving fatal but in few inftances. The general method, as has been fuggefled, has been
the moft fuccefsful in its preceeding and prefent appearance.

An Apology.

THE acknowledged fentiment that the
medical art has been improved by praƈical
obfervations of phyficians; and a compliance
with the requeft of the Maffachufetts Medical
Society to praƈitioners in general, to make obfervations on epidemics in particular, will, I
hope, be an apology for the foregoing obfervations.

𝕸𝖊𝖉𝖎𝖈𝖆𝖑 𝕾𝖐𝖊𝖙𝖈𝖍𝖊𝖘, &c.

Heat the Principle of Animation, &c.

THAT principle which chymifts and philofophers have demonftrated to exift in all bodies, is, doubtlefs, the only vivifying principle in the univerfe. This fluid has received various names according as it was combined with other elements, as electricity combined and exifting in air, phlogifton, or inflammable matter in oil and other inflamma-

ble

ble bodies, fire, heat, &c. as an element or principle of matter.*

We perceive this principle to act nearly alike on animal and vegetable bodies. It re-animates insects and other animal bodies, when life has been sufpended through the influence of cold, and vegetation lives again on the return of heat. Vegetation cannot exist without the influence of the other known elements of matter, as earth, air, and water. In the animal economy without this all vivifying and fupporting fluid, and a conftant fupply of food, containing a portion of *thefe*, he fails, fickens and dies. By the union of thefe the air becomes the principle of vitality, or the breath of life.

Salubrious or fixed air, we may fuppofe, is a compound, acting on our bodies by cer-

tain

* *Chymifts have demonftrated this principle of phlogifton to be a component part of all bodies, and only a fecondary principle, and to diftinguifh it from pure, unmixed fire, call it fire fixed or compounded with other elements.*

tain laws we do not comprehend; and is conftantly received into the lungs and inftantaneoufly decompounded, and thofe parts neceffary for life are abforbed, and the remainder exhaled as ufelefs and even deleterious.*

The univerfal, or vitriolic acid, which philofophers have demonftrated to exift in the air, which is a faline or earthy fubftance, heat and water, are components of this animating fluid.

Its mode of fupporting life we do not underftand.

We

* It has been found by Dr. HALE, that a perfon in health deftroys two gallons of air in two minutes and an half; fo as to render it unfit for refpiration.

(HALE's Statical Effays.)

Dr. PERCIVAL has difcovered that air which animals have breathed is in all refpects the fame with air in which animals have putrefied. The original quantity is diminifhed in both cafes, which is owing to the precipitation of the fixed air it contained.

D2

We may fuppofe a certain proportion of each neceffary to compofe this fluid. And alfo this principle has influence in continuing the power of cohefion in animated bodies. The caufe of putrefaction is an excefs of heat, for bodies in a putrefactive fermentation have an increafed action, heat and agitation, which decompounds the different elements and particles which compofe the body.

The principle of phlogifton alfo exifts in the various kinds of fuftenance, in a fixed ftate, as in wine, oil, fpices, and animal food, and in different degrees, as is evident from the ftrength obtained from animal, and the debility, from vegetable food.

This compound is not only the vital principle of life, it is alfo the nervous energy, the caufe of all fenfation and mufcular motion.*

" Human

* *Wine, fpirits and opium, contain a large fhare of this inflammable principle and increafe the mobility of the nervous power to a certain point, beyond that, confufion of ideas; carried farther, a difarrangement and diforganization of the brain.*

" Human life," fays a late writer, * " is
an aggregate of at leaft three ingredients—perception, intelligence, and vegetation ; and
fince man is declared to be a compound,
the natural prefumption is, that the life of this
compound being is itfelf a compound. The
mechanifm of life, which is vegetative, is
wholly of the body, and confifts of a fyme-
try and fympathy of parts and a correfpon-
dence of motions, conducive by mechanical
laws to the confervation of the whole." The
influence of air entering the pulmonary veffels, is mechanical, and when it is called the
vital principle, refers to the mechanifm of life,
in that part which belongs to the body only.
How far the vegetative life is influenced by
heat and cold, I may now confider, as this
only comes under the notice of the phyfician
and phyfiologift.

Philofophers affure us that whatever are
the properties of heat, thofe of cold are direct-

ly

* *Bifhop* HORSLEY, *before the Humane Society,* 1789.

ly oppofite. Heat flows inceffantly from the fun and is effentially fluid, and the principle of fluidity in other bodies. Cold is a privation of heat, its qualities being different; while this condenfes, that dilates. Thefe two oppofite qualities feem to produce analogous effects when carried to a certain point; for cold condenfes till after congelation, then like heat it expands the frozen fubftance.

Phyfiologifts have affigned various operations or effects from the influence of cold—and when applied in certain ftates of the body becomes an aftiingent to the furface, contracts the exhaling veffels and retains the heat which ought to be carried off by perfpiration. Various degrees have various operations according to former habits and particular ftates of the body at the time it is applied, &c.

The influence of heat is alfo various, operating according to its duration. intenfity, an l alternation with cold and moifture. Its excefs like cold becomes an aftringent; con-

tracts

tracts the surface and retains the perspiratory
fluid. It has been proved that a hot room
gives a cold, sooner than one of lower temperature; a cold being only the retention or
accumulation of heat in the system. *

It has been observed that heat is the prin-
cipal mover in the mechanism of life, the
principle of vegetative and animal motion—
but it is at the same time acknowledged that
an excess deranges and mechanically destroys
the organization of the system.‡

The heat of the body may be increased to
a certain degree without a fever's being
present; but if carried beyond the point of
evaporation, a febrile stricture takes place. In
the

* Dr. ALEXANDER *has proved that a person may be
too hot to sweat, and that there is a sweating point, and in
any degree above or below, it cannot be obtained, till the
heat is lowered by cold, or increased by heat.*

‡ Animals, even those the most tenacious of life, and
whose existence is found to depend the least on air, sooner
expire in air made foul, than in vacuo.
(LIND on fever.)

the vegetable economy, heat ftops perfpiration, equally as froft or cold.* Heat applied to the body in any confiderable degree,
produces a febrile fpafm, and a dangerous
fever enfues; heat being received into the
lungs and determined to the fkin, inflames and
irritates the nerves on the furface, and a ftricture is induced.

A modern pathologift,† fuppofes the
proximate caufe of fever is fpafm, and the re-
mote caufes are fedative or debilitating powers, &c. which acting on the primary organ,
the brain, produce a dimimifhed energy;
which has iufluence on the heart and arteries,
by weakening their force and action. This and
the *vis medicatrix naturæ*; § produce fpafm and
fever. ·The hypothefis is not eafy to be com-
prehended.

* *Plants fooner fuffer and droop beneath the influence of
noxious air, than in the want of this vivifying fluid.*
(LIND on fever.)

† *Dr.* CULLEN.

§ *It is hard to comprehend this power in the fyftem, unlefs it be reaction.*

prehended. It is hard to conceive how motion and vigor can be increafed, when their
caufe is diminifhed; or how a diminifhed influence can produce an increafed action. The
Doctor fuppofes the fpafm &c. indirectly
ftimulate the heart and arteries, and thereby
reftore energy to the brain, which has influence in obviating the atony and fpafm on the
furface.

The influence of the nerves in the brain is
continued by the conftant fupply of blood, of
agreeable motion and temperature, and the
blood flows confonantly to the energy the
heart and the arteries receive from the nerves.
Experience informs us that in almoft every
inftance of debility, when the action of the
heart is weak, the reaction is likewife; the
refiftence being in proportion to the dif-
tending force. In cafes of debility an equal
balance is obferved between the action and
reaction, and an equal diftribution of blood
to the exterior veffels. Every paroxyfm of
fever increafes debility in the various func-

tions,

tions, and at the crifis the weaknefs is greater than at any preceeding period in difeafe. On the whole the effect cannot ceafe while the caufe remains; neither can the fame power produce vigor and weaknefs.

An Hypothefis.

MAY not febrile fpafm arife from *phlogiftic* heat? an excefs being accumulated in the fyftem, may it not inflame and excite the origin of the nerves in the brain, and be immediately communicated to thofe on the furface? Heat, cold, and moifture, equally contract the diameters of the exhaling veffels, and imprifon the perfpiratory fluid, which being phlogifticated air, * and highly ftimulant, induces a febrile ftricture.

This

---

* *Heat, moifture, and ftagnated air, and human effluvia, fuch as fweat and perfpiratory matter from the fkin and lungs, are the grand promoters of putrefaction.*

(WHITE on puerpural fevers.)

This ftimulant fluid inflames and contracts the folids, and rarefies the fluids, ftim-
ulates the heart and arteries, which increafes
the heat and ftricture on the furface, and the
febrile motions commence.

Dr. Rush * writes, that in the late fever
at Philadelphia, the pulfe was increafed nearly
twenty ftrokes in a minute, in thofe who had
not a fever. A prefumption, that the caufe
was a phlogiftic atmofphere or an excefs of
ftimuli, which correfponding with a particular ftate of body, produced a febrile ftricture.
Another fact, favoring the fuppofition, is, that
neither women, nor children, were fo liable to
the difeafe as men.

The lax fibre of the former, not being fo
eafily conftricted as the latter, by the heated
atmofphere. And I may remark further, that
if real weaknefs, or diminifhed force, ftrength,
or tone of the nerves, was the caufe, why

was

* See his letter to Dr. ROGERS.

E

was the debilitating courfe, fuch as large and repeated bleedings and other evacuations, fo neceffary and falutary ? As he informs us he carried it to great excefs before the corded pulfe and other inflammatory fymptoms could be obviated ; and at the fame time omitted all kinds of tonic or ftimulant medicines.

Febrile Symptoms.

THE firft febrile influence, it has been fuppofed, is on the brain ; but from fympathy and a peculiar fenfibility of the ftomach, a perception, very unpleafant and difagreeable, is firft noticed in that organ ; it arifes from excefs of ftimuli in the fyftem, and begins to operate while the fpafm is forming.

The fucceeding fymptom is debility, which is a falfe perception ; the whole vafcular fyftem being in a ftate of febrile tenfion and fpafm ; which ftate produces a fenfation

of

of cold, which is not real, but apparent only ; for the fufferer is under more than ufual
heat except at the extremities.* The fymptom following is increafed heat ; and the paroxyfm which enfues, is a mechanical effort
of the heart and arteries, and the expanfive
force of the rarefied air and fluids ; and the
febrile refiftance on the furface ; which effort
is continued till a diftribution is made to the
furface, and a partial relaxation is obtained,
and a portion of heat carried off by exhalation.

Contagion is phlogiftic air, arifing from
human or other putrifying bodies, being greatly concentrated, and joined with acrimonious
falts

---

* By feveral experiments made by Dr. HOME, in the
cold and even fhivering fit of an intermittent, it appeared
that the heat of the patient, by FARENHEITS' thermometer,
was 104 degrees, whereas that of a perfon in health feldom
exceeds 98.

During the cold fit of an ague, the heat is confiderably
increafed.
(LIND's Appendix.)

falts and oil of the putrifying fubftance ;
which violently ftimulate the nervous fyftem,
and if received into the fyftem, produce febrile fpafm. It may be fuppofed that air decompounded, or that has paffed the lungs and
bodies of animals, as that in jails, hofpitals,
&c. is not materially different from that arifing from dried brooks and ftagnant water;
the water, air, and acid, being•feperated, its
falubrity and vivifying power is deftroyed.
The excitement, which this imprifoned and
contagious fluid gives to the fyftem, is very
great—as anxiety, naufea, horror, cold, fhivering, thirft, headache, delirium, and other
preternatural irritations.

Its activity with certain ftates of heat, has,
likewife, immediate morbid effects on the fluids, by decompounding and deftroying the
globular fyftem of the blood. Its ftimulant
qualities deftroy the affinity of the various elements in compound, and break the union or
relation each bore to the other. The putrefactive ftate commences, and the elements
affume their original ftate. The

The intermitting fever is different from all others, and may be confidered as an aptitude or tendency to a febrile ftate. This fever, only, is under the control of medicine, and if neglected, difcovers a tendency to a remitting or continued fever. An apparent crifis fuceeeds the paroxyfm, as appears by the general relaxation and natural excretions from the furface. After a certain period or intermiffion of certain duration, according to the original type and tendency, the fame phenomena are renewed.

In the foregoing fketches it is fuppofed, that animal life has, in fome refpects, an analogy with vegetative, and that the influence of heat and cold is analagous, that heat or phlogifton is the caufe of fpafm, when an excefs is accumulated, and that this active principle decompounds the air, and other fluids. The hypothefis being admitted, ftill no new indications can be fuggefted, unlefs it fhould be, an admiffion of cold air and drink. Thefe, it is acknowledged, are allowed by every

ery, practitioner of eminence; but I would
afk with deference to thofe of more experience and information, whether cold bathing
and air, &c. might not be as fafe and ufeful,
in fome fevers of this climate, as in thofe
of Jamaica? Which practice Dr. JACKSON
ftrongly recommends, from much experience,
both in the Weft-Indies and England. No-
fologifts have multiplied the names of fevers,
defignating according to the local determination, or prevailing fymptom, as putred, yellow, nervous, &c. &c. yet we have reafon to
fuppofe the caufe is effentially the fame, but
the tendency different.

I conclude by introducing an inftance of
the effect of cold in an inflammatory fever.—
A perfon now living in this place was violently attacked with a pleurify, and almoft from
the commencement became delirious; on the
feventh day of difeafe, the watcher falling to
fleep, the patient rofe from bed and travelled
into the garden adjoining the houfe; and being entangled with potatoe vines, fell down
and

lay fome time, at leaft, till he became very cold ; the watcher finding his patient gone ; after confiderable fearch with a light difcovered him as related, perfectly reftored to reafon—was affifted back to bed—foon became warm and flept eafily. His fever and adventure terminated together.

A SUMMARY OF THE FOREGOING INDUCTIONS—WITH REMARKS.

THE vegetative life of man requires a conftant fupply of air of certain temperature, and which fupports life by refpiration and evaporation from the furface ; and that the caufe of fever is an excefs of this animating principle ; and febrile fpafm is an effect of its exciting power ; and that this power or principle may be accumulated in the body from external cold, heat, or moifture, or be imbibed from contagious exhalations, arifing from putrefying animals or vegetables ; which ftate never commences till the air is decompounded, and

its

its falubrity deftroyed, and that this heated
fluid may be unequally diftributed and determined, and produce all the various phenomena
in fevers ; if to the brain and nervous fyftem, a
nervous—to the inteftines, putrid and dyfenter-
ic—to the biliary fyftem and liver, bilious and
yellow fever, &c. &c. This electric principle
may be locally exerted on a particular part,
and produce great pain and irritation as foon
as the fpafm is formed, and evaporation ceaf-
es—as in rheumatifm, felons, &c. The hypothefis is farther fupported by the ufe of me-
tallic points, lately introduced by Dr. PER-
KINS, in curing local inflammations, &c. By
thefe mineral conductors, the inflammable
principle is attracted and carried off. Refpectable characters have given teftimony of their
utility.—However, we may fuppofe the heat
cannot be conducted out of the body in any
confiderable degree, without fome evacuation
of the fluids ; as by perfpiration, bleeding,
purging, &c. but we have unequivocal proof
that the application of cold deftroys and overcomes its ftimulant power, as in burns, &c.

alfo

alfo in fever's being relieved without any vi-
fible evacuation—one inftance in the memoirs
of Baron Trenk, by drinking cold water. I
have only to remark, that I have lately cured
fevers, by warm bathing and cold drink, when
the moft celebrated febrifuges had failed.

P. S. As a farther illuftration that febrile ftricture is the effect of heated air accumulated in the fyftem from accidental caufes;
I here fubjoin a few cafes from Dr. Jackson's
notes, on the ufe and fafety of cold bathing.

" As the cold bathing, which I have fo
ftrongly recommended in the cure of fevers,
has an exterior appearance of being a rafh
and hazardous remedy, I fhall relate fome cafes which may enable the reader to judge more
precifely of its real effects.

" The firft hints I had of this practice were
accidental, and arofe from a converfation I
had with the mafter of a veffel, in which I
went paffenger. As he was talking one day
of the ftate of the fleet, he mentioned acci-
dentally,

dentally, that fome men were fent aboard his
fhip ill of fevers; feveral of whom, jumped
into the fea during the delirium which attended the paroxfyms of difeafe. Some of them
were drowned—but thofe who recovered from
the waves, 'appeared to be greatly benefited
by the ducking. I was refolved to bring it
to the teft of experiment, as foon as oppor-
tunity fhould offer. A poor failor was the
firft whofe fituation feemed to juftify fuch a
trial. He had been ill two days; the delirium ran high; his eyes were red and inflamed;
his refpiration was hurried; he was anxious
and reftlefs in a high degree, whilft together
with thofe marks of excitement, he was occa-
fionally languid and difpofed to faint. His
fkin being dirty furnifhed an oftenfible excufe
for trying this remedy. But it was previoufly
thought proper to draw fome blood from the
arm; which being done, fome buckets of falt
water were dafhed on the fhoulders. He was
now laid in bed; a copious fweat enfued; fucceeded by a diftinct remiffion, and a total
change in the nature of the fymptoms.

The

The fuccefs I met with in this inftance was more than I had expected; I was therefore encouraged to try the fame mode of bathing in a perfon who came under my care fome weeks after, and who had been ill of a fever fix or feven days. This patient had been bled and bliftered;—emetics and cathartics had been likewife employed, and bark had been given in the ufual manner, for the three laft days. The fever however, had now in a great manner loft its type. The man was low and languid; his eyes were dim; his vifion indiftinct; his pulfe fmall and frequent, and, when the head was raifed from the pillow, not to be felt. Though it did not appear that he could reafonably be expected to live long, I ftill wifhed to get him conveyed to the deck, that a trial might be made of the effect of cold bathing; but the fituation was fo ticklifh, that I felt fome uneafinefs in getting about it. At laft he was lifted through the hatch way in a blanket, though I muft confefs that I was not without apprehenfions that he might die under my hands. Some wine was

then

then poured down his throat; and he was
fprinkled with cold falt water as he lay upon
the deck.

Appearing to be fomewhat invigorated by
this procefs, he was raifed up very gently,
and feveral buckets of the fea water were
dafhed about his head and fhoulders. He
was then laid in bed; the pulfe foon became
large and full. I left him in a copious fweat
and was agreeably furprifed next day to find
him fitting on the deck, to which he had
walked on his own feet.

Another inftance, in which the effects of
cold bathing were more decifive than in the
former. A boy, aged fourteen, had been ill
of a fever feven or eight days. Nothing had
been omitted in point of treatment, which is
ufual to be done in fimilar cafes. Bark and
wine had been carried as far as could be fer-
vicable, or even fafe; yet death feemed to be
approaching faft. The fuccefs of cold bathing, in fome inftances fimilar to the prefent,
fo far exceeded my expectation, that I was
induced

induced to make trial of it, in the cafe before me, tho I was not without apprehenfions that death might be the confequence of the attempt. The bufinefs, however was accomplifhed without accident; and next day the boy was able, not only to fit up in bed, but even to walk over the floor.

"After inftances fo unequivocal as the above, it would be fuperfluous to mention any others. I fhall only add, that I have tried the remedy in various fituations, always with fafety, generally with aftonifhing fuccefs; fo that I cannot forbear recommending it even at an early period in fevers. It communicates tone and vigor to the powers of life, and diminifhes irritability in a degree far fuperior to all other cordials or fedatives.

" The bathing was managed in the following manner : the water which was required to be of a refiefhing degree of coolnefs, was dafhed by means of a bucket on

F   the

the head and fhoulders.　It was found, likewife that its good effects were heightened,
in fome cafes, by previous bleeding, and by
the previous ufe of warm bathing."

E R R A T A.